A GUIDE TO MAKING TAX DIGITAL

A GUIDE
TO MAKING TAX DIGITAL

LINDA JANE HODGSON

Greenwich Exchange
London

Greenwich Exchange, London

First published in Great Britain in 2022
All rights reserved

A Guide to Making Tax Digital
© Linda Jane Hodgson, 2022

Printed and bound by imprintdigital.com
Cover design by December Publications
Tel: 07951511275

Greenwich Exchange website: www.greenex.co.uk

Cataloguing in Publication Data
is available from the British Library

ISBN: 978-1-910996-66-9

CONTENTS

1

What's Making Tax Digital All About?

Benjamin Franklin is quoted as saying there are two things certain in life: 'Death and Taxes' and, in fact, in Inheritance Tax you may have both.

I would hazard to add there are two things certain in modern life: 'Digital Technology and Taxes' and in Making Tax Digital you do have both.

Nobody likes paying taxes. However, it is a burden which most people will accept as a way of financing society although we may well differ in our opinions as to how the tax money should be spent and allocated. The later debate lies within the region of politics and will not be our concern here, however. What will be our concern is ensuring that we, the taxpayers, pay the right amount of tax with as little hassle as possible.

Having established then that tax may be our adversary

to some extent, we need to deal with it as effectively as possible in order to enjoy a relatively trouble free, if not tax-free, existence. Although keeping too close company alongside an adversary is not recommended, keeping an adversary at bay is sometimes necessary. However, we will only be considering here legally accepted measures and that is what this little book is all about in essence.

From April 2019 a new system for the assessment of tax called Making Tax Digital was brought into existence in the UK. What this means, in effect, is that the Government replaces the previous self-assessment system with an online tax accounts system recorded digitally.

This system of Digital Account takes a few years to be phased in. So, we do have time to become adjusted to it, but we need to do it now and essentially this book explains what to do.

This is a major change in some respects, and it has major administrative and other implications for the Revenue and Customs. That is also not really our major concern here, however. What we want to know is what are the differences for us, the taxpayers, from the previous systems. Basically, they are very few.

Firstly: Will the amount of tax we pay be changed? No, not due to Making Tax Digital. Although yearly Budgets and changes embodied in the yearly Finance Acts passed by the Goverrnment through Parliament do make changes to the tax we pay, but they do this already and this is not due to Digital Taxation.

Secondly: Will the times of payment be changed? Yes, most likely payment may be quicker and more frequent for some types of taxes and systems but still within the requirements of the laws passed by Parliament. One of the reasons for Making Tax Digital is to make the system more efficient and quicker. It is already accepted that the self-employed have a longer delay in the payment of their Income Tax than say the employees who pay taxes under the very upfront Pay as You Earn System. This was known as one of the attractions of being self-employed as opposed to being an employee. In fact, under PAYE the employee does not even have a chance to lay their hands on their own tax payment. It is deducted from the pay packet before they even see it, so they receive only their NET pay.

Thirdly: Will the location of the Tax Office be changed? Yes, it will be online linked to your software system and your Bank.

Fourthly: Will I become liable to tax if I wasn't liable before? No, it should not change your tax status.

Fifthly: Will I have to buy a new computer, take a training course, or obtain a Degree in Maths? No, but see below.

Sixthly: So, what will change for me? You will have to acquire Making Tax Digital software which has been HMRC approved. You have probably seen all the advertisements for this MTD software. Various brands are in competition for your custom. You must choose an

HMRC approved brand, and it will be linked to your Bank account details.

Your accountant, if you have one, will also have access to the information you enter onto the software.

Seventhly: So, will I be required to keep financial records? Yes, you already are required to do this by law as a taxpayer. The difference in Making Tax Digital is that the software will automatically keep the records for you once you have entered the details. Both you and HMRC will have access and your accountant if you have one. The software will also be populated by information held by HMRC.

Finally: Will I be required to comply with the new system? Yes, unless you have digital exemption (see next chapter). You are required to comply. Non-compliance can result in addictional charges being placed on you by HMRC.

BASICALLY, THAT'S IT.

2

When Will This New System Apply?

Making Tax Digital is phased in gradually. As you are no doubt aware there are several different taxes operating in the UK. They each have a slightly different timetable for when Making Tax Digital is introduced.

Value Added Tax (VAT)

Value Added Tax (VAT) is an Indirect Tax which is basically a Sales Tax and is collected in by the trader, not the customer, although it is the end customer who pays it. That end customer does not have direct contact with HMRC about VAT, however. It is only the trader that has the contact with HMRC over VAT and sends in the VAT Return and the tax due. Hence it is called an Indirect Tax.

Making Tax Digital already applies to VAT to some extent and is extended to all VAT registered businesses.

So, VAT registered businesses must acquire the HMRC approved software and have it linked to their Bank account details. This can be done by the business itself or assisted by their accountant. Remember VAT applies to both VAT registered sole traders and companies. The tax is calculated by means of adding the OUTPUT VAT payments collected in from Customers and deducting any INPUT VAT paid by the businesses on paying out on purchases and other allowable expenses and Capital payments.

The rules for the registration of a business for VAT depend on the business TURNOVER or sales threshold and whether the products are VAT standard rated, reduced rate, zero rated or exempt as they do already, subject to change by Budgets and Government Legislation.

Registered Businesses selling VAT-rated goods (NOT exempt goods) with TURNOVER above the threshold have been required to operate Making Tax Digital since April 2019. Following on from this, all businesses selling VAT-rated goods (NOT exempt goods), notwithstanding whether the business turnover was above or below the threshold, had to comply with Making Tax Digital from April 2022.

Income Tax

Many of us are employees and pay our Income Tax on our EARNINGS on a receipts basis through the PAYE system. We have a Contract of Employment. Our Employer calculates our tax according to our Code Number and it is taken directly out of our pay packet so that all we receive is our net pay after tax. This will not change in the foreseeable future, and we are the least likely to be affected by Making Tax Digital.

However, you are probably aware that self-employed taxpayers (not companies) and taxpayers with income from property pay Income Tax on their PROFITS, not Turnover nor their earnings and are not subject to the PAYE SYSTEM for the payment of their tax. PROFITS are calculated basically by adding assessable business income for a period and deducting allowable expenses related to the same period. Various rules apply to this calculation of profits which is not necessarily our concern here. Basically, these rules are not changed by Making Tax Digital.

However, self-employed taxpayers and taxpayers with income from property will be required under the new rules to use Making Tax Digital compliant accounting software to record their income and expenditure and to update their digital accounts every three months.

Making Tax Digital for the self-employed and landlords is likely to come into being first for those businesses with an annual gross income of over £10,000 or a similar figure from 6 April 2024, and later for all businesses and landlords. The way they pay their tax may well change.

However, it is likely there will be exemptions, and some

taxpayers may be digitally excluded on the grounds of age, religion, disability, or location.

Corporation Tax (CT)

Making Tax Digital will also apply to Corporation Tax paid by companies but will follow the introduction of MTD for Income Tax and will probably be introduced in 2026 or later.

3

Where And How Can I Get Help?

There is no need to rush out and buy arms full of expensive books, computer programmes, and the like, although the market is full of such things. However, you will need some materials to assist you.

Firstly, Making Tax Digital does require that you buy some MAKING TAX DIGITAL HMRC computer software. There are several good products on the market, and it is worth researching the different ones and getting something that is recommended to you maybe by a friend, colleague, accountant, or your Bank. It must be HMRC approved, however.

You will not need complicated calculators or mathematical equipment to work out your tax. A clear head, your records, and recording and communication materials are probably all that is required with possibly the assistance of your accountant if you already have one.

My advice is not to dismiss your accountant on the grounds that Making Tax Digital and the software will do it all for you. Although it is said that the software is intended to help us and make the job of tax paying easier, people have found that there are quite a few pitfalls along the way. Each case is slightly different, and the accountant will have much more experience of how it all works than you do. Remember that the system is only as good as the information you put into it. Yes, the system links to your Bank Account and will tally in that way. However, what about receipts that didn't get banked or expenditure that was paid out in Cash?

The advice would be to keep your own records and copies of all that is sent and entered, received and paid out, or due to be received or paid out in the time frame you are working with, to check everything or get someone else to do this for you. Records made at the time of a transaction are invaluable. They don't have to be fancy, just recorded at the time or not long afterwards. If figures are estimated by you then someone can challenge that estimate and do a better job. It is very hard, however, to challenge an original record made at the time.

Mistakes can still happen, investigations can take place and you need to be ready with answers, original documents and dates recorded.

I remember an occasion when teaching a Computerised Accounting package to students who had no knowledge of how to do manual double-entry book-keeping. The computer package asked them whether a particular entry was a Debit or a Credit. They had no knowledge of how to tell the difference and consequently there were very many mistakes. Teaching how to use the package required the teaching of basic double-entry book-keeping skills first, otherwise it just would not work successfully.

> So do not forget the basics, stick to the original rules of record keeping and double checking, then the software entries will be based on a sure footing of stone and not on moveable sand, sticks, and straw, and you can face any challenge.

4

What Records Do I Need Then?

Even a gangster as untouchable as Al Capone can be defeated in the end by his tax records or his lack of them. If you keep no records or very few of your financial affairs, you leave yourself open to the estimates and speculations of others who do not necessarily have your best interests at heart. On the other hand, if you can lay your hands on records of what money you have received and how it has been spent or saved, who can argue with you?

Your records are there to help you not to hinder you. It may seem tedious to have to bother but just recall how great it is to lay your hands on that missing receipt that allows you to claim a shopping refund or your payslip that allows you to claim back tax overpaid. The things you need to keep records of are:

1. All the income you receive IN A CERTAIN TIME PERIOD, USUALLY A TAX YEAR FROM 6 APRIL TO THE

FOLLOWING 5 APRIL including wages, salaries, royalties, interest, allowances, benefits, pensions, commissions, self-employed payments in, overtime, bonuses, ... this list can go on and on and on. It is not exhaustive because there are always many, many different words and forms of money coming in. Do not worry whether it is taxable or not at this stage. Keep a record anyway: IF YOU RECEIVE IT, RECORD IT.

2. All your expenditure should also be recorded, especially if it relates to your business. If you are not sure it is best to record it. These payments include cash, cheque, direct debit, credit card, and all internet payments.

Try to keep your business and personal expenses separate if possible as HMRC will always be on the lookout for this. Repairs to business premises and your personal home may have been undertaken by the same workmen and you may have paid only one bill, but they do need to be separated for tax purposes. One part will be allowable and the other will not, but the accountant can help you with this even if the software does not. Again, best to record everything, it can always be eliminated later. IF YOU PAY IT, RECORD IT.

5

Suppose I Get It Wrong?

We all make mistakes sometimes and Revenue and Customs do not expect its customers to be perfect. However, it will expect them to be honest.

If a mistake occurs and comes to your knowledge it is possible to correct it in the light of new information or genuine errors. There are also important RIGHTS OF APPEAL. They are, however, covered by strict deadlines and guidelines, and it is important to be aware of these rights.

Rights are usually printed on official documentation or covered by website information. It is important to start early and read about them at the beginning and not afterwards. It is no defence to say you didn't know when it has been plainly notified. If you are in business or hold a position of authority, ignorance is not usually a defence unless you can prove you were unable to act due to illness or disability. So late appeal procedures are there but can only be used if you can produce some evidence to support your cause. 'Not bothering' is usually not good enough.

It is usually possible to make estimates where actual figures are not known. However, beware, if you deliberately underestimate you are likely to be charged interest and possibly penalties on any late payment due as a result of your underestimation.

However, it should be said here that Making Tax Digital is intended to prevent the need for such cat and mouse estimates by making figures recorded at the time of payment or agreement to pay, they eliminate the estimation factor. Figures become derived from real time recordings rather than best guess estimates in the dark. Moreover, the figures are already with HMRC through the digital software and mechanisms so in some cases, although not all, there is no need to submit anything.

If you like, it is playing the role of a SMART METER for the tax system!

So, all this means there is less opportunity for you to go wrong or get it wrong. Just like with a Smart Meter you do not have to go and read your meter, nor does the electricity supplier.

This is not to say, of course, that things can never go wrong. Machines break down too or malfunction or their input or installation was just not good enough. However, mistakes are much less likely to happen in the normal course of things and this is one of the whole points to the system. Upfront and faultless if not quite so.

Of course, HMRC is only peopled and invented by humans also and sometimes does make mistakes in systems and judgements. Therefore, you should never totally take your eye off the ball or off the road. Auditing and checking are still very important functions.

If something looks wrong, it probably is. Fraud, a deliberate attempt to deceive for gain, can exist in any system. In the Revenue they used to look to see if claims made on paper had had the paper folded. If it had been folded it was likely to have come in the post inside an envelope smaller than itself. If it was on unfolded paper, how had it reached them? It could be an internal fraudulent claim on office paper.

6

Can I Survive All This Alone?

The new system has been designed to make the tax system simpler and more accessible to everyone, so yes, in theory, you can survive alone. However, most people don't or choose not to do so.

There are many professional bodies who are willing and able to assist you, for a charge, of course, and you will have already had to have the expense of buying the DIGITAL HMRC APPROVED SOFTWARE.

The accounting profession will not decrease in size or go out of business as a result of this system. It may even become enlarged. Accountants will still be needed to prepare accounts and returns and may even manage and operate the software for you, under your authority, of course.

There will also be a lot of free advice on government

and other advisory websites. As with filing a Tax Return, one good guidebook or website is often invaluable. However, make sure you know whether any advice is free or not, or what the terms are before you engage. Some tax advice can be tremendously expensive. A few basic hints:

1. Always follow any guidelines or advice given by HMRC. If they suggest opening two bank accounts: one for business, one for private payments, do so without question. They very rarely challenge their own advice.

2. If you already have an accountant, keep them on and if you do not have an accountant think of engaging one. They will know a lot about the new system and have seen many more pitfalls.

3. Keep records of all your financial transactions as they occur. Don't make the mistake of being lazy or leaving things out. Invoices going out are numbered and the Revenue will seek a reason for any missing ones.

4. Make sure the records are not too vague. Keep details and original documents so that you can prove dates and names and quantities. 'Some money spent on materials' is a useless record and probably would not be allowed to be claimed. How much money, when, to whom, for which materials, and for what purpose? The what, why, when, how, who, questions all need to be answered and not vaguely.

5. Don't enter vague uncertified figures: £100 for this, £200 for that. Expenses and income are rarely like that.

For example, it is £124.60, most likely, and needs to be accurate and verifiable.

6. Always meet deadlines AND KNOW WHAT THEY ARE IN ADVANCE. Even if figures are correct, out of date figures may not be accepted by HMRC.

7. Don't panic. Usually matters can be put right, although it may cost you. Better to get it right from the beginning if you can.

7

What If They Disagree With Me?

HMRC can, and will, conduct investigations into tax liabilities. It is, if you like, a policing system to ensure that the whole procedure works correctly and that there is no abuse of the system. Such investigations will continue – we have no information that they will not.

If your tax affairs are selected for investigation, it is important to keep your head, and work with the Revenue, not against them. It may feel as though you may be being accused wrongly and the only solution is to run away and keep running just one step ahead of the Authorities. However, the best solution is to face the music and dance with it.

Investigation may mean simply that certain items or amounts need to be clarified. Your records may not have been as full and reliable as they should have been, and the Revenue may want to agree alterations or amendments with you. This system can, in fact, be seen as quite helpful, even if it results in more tax. It gets you on the right lines for the future. You can see it as a form of advice although HMRC do not usually give it this name or call it this as such.

However, HMRC will see investigations very much in this light especially early years new business investigations. Always take on board HMRC guidelines even if not called advice. When challenged you can always refer to this guidance. Some underpayments of tax can be collected by means of an adjustment to your PAYE Code Number, so you pay off any debt each month and spread the financial burden that way.

Other tax liabilities may have to be paid straight away and it is better to do so otherwise they may attract interest, but the Revenue can help with financial arrangements for such payments. It is always best to pay part of a bill if you cannot pay the whole amount. The Revenue rarely refuses to accept payment, and this will put a halt to any proceedings already undertaken by them to collect the whole amount.

The whole intention of the new Making Tax Digital system is to make the whole system more current, visible, and up front, so to speak. Backlogs of tax are less likely to happen once the whole system is underway. Part of the Revenue's job is to educate its customers as to the new system and to ensure it runs smoothly. It does have advantages for you in the long run, although there are initial extra costs. Better to embrace it than fight it. The Revenue usually appreciates a co-operative approach.

Also, you are entitled to expect and ask for customer service from the Revenue, and if you ask for help and clarification you should receive it. Beware of asking for a bland 'I should like all my tax affairs reviewed please'. The unexpected may turn up. Best to leave well alone. A specific query may be helpful, however.

In other words, the system intends to be one of co-operation rather than fugitive and pursuer. You may be a highly intelligent fugitive and feel you should not be pursued at all. However, the Revenue will have a highly-trained and persistent investigator who is no fool either, and sooner or later you two may meet, even if your accountant comes along too. It is better if the meeting is sooner rather than later, on your own terms, and with as much goodwill and respect as possible.

8

How Do I Know What I Owe?

If you have been investigated by the Revenue, although this is very unlikely even for most of us, you may have been invited to an interview. This may seem a very daunting experience and you may have taken your accountant along with you.

There will always be notes or records of such meetings and certainly follow up communications to confirm any agreements made. These will be signed and dated, and you should check to see that the communications agree with your own recollections of what was agreed. If they do not, then say so.

For most of us there will be no investigation. Details of what we owe will come to us in the form of electronic communications. Again, it is important to check these. If you receive a statement, it should show you what is due, what has been paid, and what is still owing.

Tax documents are important. They need to be checked and often retained. Mistakes do happen and you may need to have them corrected. Many people who have paid Income Tax under PAYE will have known the value of having kept a P45 or P60 document so that either one could go from one job to another in a seamless fashion in a tax context or so that refund of tax could be obtained during the tax year or after it had ended. Official tax documents are valuable, and I would always save your own documents for six years – the same period that you are required to keep access to your business records.

Checking is important. There is a whole auditing profession devoted to checking internally within organisations and externally. Several great organisations that have fallen by the wayside were shown to have shortcomings in auditing practices. You should do your own personal and business checking too. Checking Bank statements and Tax statements is imperative.

Mistakes are sometimes made, and it is hoped that they can be easily corrected early on. It is intended that Making Tax Digital will reduce errors and enable them to be corrected quickly and automatically. However, your own simple checking system involving original documents is invaluable. You only need to look at a few recent cases where computer system errors have been blamed on individuals operating the systems, but innocent of the mistakes, such as in the case of the Sub Post Office workers.

There was also a recent case of a trader's so-called

missing VAT purchase invoices because there was a gap in the numbering sequence of the invoices, and it was assumed they had been lost and missed out or not existed and the amount the trader had claimed for them was not allowed. However, the trader in question was reluctant to accept this conclusion since he was a meticulous record keeper. He appealed against the additional assessment and found the original invoice documents. They had been on very flimsy paper in the first place which had stuck together with the invoices around them after being numbered. So, the missing invoices did exist and, once traced, the amounts could be allowed and were in time because of the appeal.

9

Will The New System Play Fair?

Customer service and Customer satisfaction are thought to be watchwords of the new system as well as it being a system which is more efficient and transparent. It is meant to be clearer and more accessible to the taxpayer, but it is also fair to say that the taxpayer is going to have to put more effort and cost into making it work.

PAYE is said to have made unpaid tax collectors out of employers, and VAT has made unpaid tax collectors out of traders and businesses. Making Tax Digital is in danger of making unpaid tax collectors out of us all and this is a big and significant advantage for the Revenue.

To make it all work, however, the Revenue must put itself across not as a giant bully or taxation Big Brother but as a responsible organisation maintaining standards of fairness and efficiency, much like other large organisations in today's economy but more so because the Revenue has much greater powers under the law and practice than those other organisations.

Although you may not have heard of it there is, in fact, an HMRC Charter. This has not just come about as a result of Making Tax Digital, but it could be argued it will be even more relevant now that tax may be swifter and more efficiently assessed.

These are the terms of the Charter:

The taxpayer can expect that HMRC will:

◆ Provide services that are accessible, easy and quick to use, at minimum cost.

◆ Be responsive, answer questions quickly, and rectify any mistakes as soon as possible.

◆ Work to make sure that everyone pays the right amount of tax.

◆ Assume that taxpayers are telling the truth unless there is evidence to the contrary.

◆ Take firm action against those who bend or break the law.

◆ Be aware of the taxpayer's personal situation and provide support if necessary.

◆ Protect taxpayer information and use that information fairly and lawfully.

◆ Treat the taxpayer with respect.

In return HMRC expects taxpayers to give full, accurate, and timely answers when asked for information and treat HMRC staff with respect.

As stated earlier, this Charter is not newly produced because of Making Tax Digital. However, you should be aware that under MTD the Revenue will be able to know about your business transactions as soon as you do, and they are entered on your Digital Software. This makes everything much sharper and keener. Firm action against those who break or bend the law may well be taken much sooner than before.

You may be aware that Tax Evasion is illegal although Tax Avoidance may not be. We may describe Avoidance as going round a tax puddle so as not to step in it (like living in, or registering your business in another country) but Evasion is a deliberate attempt to deceive (like registering your business in a hole in the wall facility in a Tax Haven outside the UK but effectively holding all meetings and administrative decision-making functions in London).

If there is a deliberate deceit for gain, (like deliberately understating profits to pay less tax) it could be Fraud which can carry a prison sentence.

You can expect to see many more activities from the Revenue on these fronts, especially on the Avoidance front. Abusive Avoidance is seen as a fair target now. There is now the GAAR, General Anti-Abuse Rule, which enables the Revenue to act against Abusive Avoidance.

Sensible arrangement of a taxpayer's affairs to minimise liability is legal and is known as Tax Planning. Splitting a company's accounts artificially so that most profits are attributed to say, USA activities, because it is the mother company and tax is paid in the USA where tax rates are lower, while most business is, in fact, done in the UK where tax rates are higher, is Abusive Avoidance and the Revenue might well act against it. Several famous international Coffee Serving and Internet Communications Businesses are said to have carried out these practices.

So, giving 'full accurate and timely answers' carries a lot of weight.

10

What's The Bottom Line Then?

There is no choice for us as to whether Making Tax Digital will apply or not. It will apply and has already done so for some taxes like VAT.

So, for us it is a matter of getting on board and understanding it as well as we can.

Once we come to terms with it, get over the initial cost of obtaining the software, I think it is manageable but if you have engaged an accountant already, I would keep them on.

There is plenty of online literature available and I would always go with the Revenue Guidelines because they are a safeguard and can be quoted back at the Revenue in times of difficulty, although the Revenue will always say the responsibility is yours, not theirs, or even your accountant's.

Remember the Charter, though. Procedure is important. Appeals are there to be used if you do not agree with something and if you behave reasonably, it always bodes well in official proceedings. Don't be afraid to plead your own case in a reasonable way. Remember the trader with the missing invoices. (Chapter Eight).

Ignorance of the system is, however, unfortunately no excuse for not taking part, which is why you need to be both forewarned and forearmed and that essentially is what this little book is attempting to do for you.

QUIZ AND ANSWERS

SOME MULTIPLE CHOICE QUESTIONS

Choose One Appropriate Answer for Each Question:

1. A Tax Haven is:

    a.   An inexpensive holiday destination.

    b.   A country where tax rates are low or non-existent.

    c.   A place where there is a sunny warm beach.

    d.   A friendly country that welcomes UK investment.

2. MTD stands for:

    a.   Micro Taxation Delivery.

    b.   Multi Tax Digitalisation.

    c.   Making Tax Digital.

    d.   Micro Tax Data.

3. Which of the following Taxes will not have MTD applied to them?

    a.   Value Added Tax.

    b.   Income Tax.

    c.   Corporation Tax.

    d.   Super Tax.

4. Which Government Office assesses and collects taxes?

   a. The Treasury.

   b. HMRC.

   c. The Home Office.

   d. The Foreign Office.

5. MTD requires the taxpayer to:

   a. Use HMRC approved software.

   b. Engage an accountant.

   c. Use HMRC approved hardware.

   d. None of the above.

6. Which of the following is Not Illegal?

   a. Avoidance of Tax.

   b. Evasion of Tax.

   c. Fraud.

   d. Concealing a source of income.

7. The HMRC Charter:

   a. Has been abolished.

   b. Never existed.

   c. Does not apply to Digital Taxation.

   d. None of the above.

8. HMRC approved Software for Digital Taxation:

    a.   Will be available to all for free.

    b.   Can only be obtained from accountants.

    c.   May be a cost to the taxpayer.

    d.   May be used or not as the taxpayer wishes.

9. As a result of MTD tax rates will:

    a.   Increase.

    b.   Decrease.

    c.   Stay the same.

    d.   Cease to exist.

10. Which records are not required by HRMC to be kept by the taxpayer for VAT purposes?

    a.   business and accounting records.

    b.   a VAT account.

    c.   a copy of each invoice issued.

    d.   invoices for payments of £25 or less for car park charges.

11. Records that are required to be kept by HMRC for VAT purposes should be kept for:

    a.   Six years or a lesser period if allowed by HMRC.

b.   Six months.

c.   One year.

d.   Three years.

12. The tax year extends from:

a.   5 April to 6 April.

b.   1 April to 31 March.

c.   6 April to 5 April.

d.   1 January to 31 December.

13. MTD will have the following effect on the tax year:

a.   No effect.

b.   It will extend it to a two-year period.

c.   It will extend it to an 18-month period.

d.   It will reduce it to a six-month period.

14. Recent anti-Evasion and anti-Abusive Avoidance legislation introduced by HMRC does not include:

a.   DOTAS (Disclosure of Tax Avoidance Schemes)

b.   GAAR (General Anti-Abuse rule)

c.   IR35 (Personal Service Company Legislation)

d.   ISAs (Individual Savings Accounts Legislation)

15. MTD will abolish the need for:

   a. Tax records.

   b. Appeals.

   c. Investigations.

   d. None of the above.

16. Under MTD engaging an accountant is in all cases:

   a. Advisable.

   b. Compulsory.

   c. Not allowed.

   d. Essential.

17. MTD will be implemented to all relevant taxes within:

   a. Six months.

   b. Within the next few years.

   c. Within a year.

   d. No fixed time limits.

18. Which of the following is not true?

   a. Digital tax accounts are set to replace all self-assessment tax returns.

   b. Digital tax accounts will apply to self-employed taxpayers and landlords.

   c.   Taxpayers will be required to update their digital tax accounts at quarterly intervals.

   d.   Taxpayers will not be required to keep electronic records of their income and expenditure.

19. Which of the following is not true?

   a.   MTD is not expected to apply to Companies and CT.

   b.   Online Digital Accounts are to be introduced for companies.

   c.   Online Digital Accounts will replace the Corporation Tax Return.

   d.   In general Companies will be required to update their accounts quarterly.

20. Which statement is not correct?

   a.   Under MTD taxpayers will be able to visit their Digital Tax Accounts accounts at any time.

   b.   Digital Tax Accounts will be pre-populated with information already held by HMRC.

   c.   In many cases there will be no need to submit any information to HMRC.

   d.   Taxpayers with income from property will be excluded from MTD legislation.

ANSWERS TO MULTIPLE CHOICE QUESTIONS

Advice: Try the questions first without reference to the answers. Then check them. You may do very well and feel you don't need much help. That is excellent. However, the Guidebook has a lot of advice as well as answers so you may find the way ahead more trouble free and, dare we say, less taxing with it, rather than without it.

ANSWERS:

1.   b
2.   c
3.   d
4.   b
5.   a
6.   a
7.   d
8.   c
9.   c
10.   d
11.   a
12.   c
13.   a

14. d
15. d
16. a
17. b
18. d
19. a
20. d